A Field of Nopes

JAMES DUCAT

BAMBOO DART PRESS

LOS ANGELES † NEW YORK † LONDON † MELBOURNE

A Field of Nopes by James Ducat

978-1-947240-41-4   Paperback
978-1-947240-42-1   eBook

Copyright © 2024 James Ducat. All rights reserved.

Cover Art by Dennis Callaci and James Ducat

Layout and design by Mark Givens

For information:

Bamboo Dart Press

chapbooks@bamboodartpress.com

Bamboo Dart Press 045

www.pelekinesis.com

www.bamboodartpress.com

SHRiMPER
www.shrimperrecords.com

This book is dedicated to my father, who convinced me to continue being an adjunct professor when I wanted to quit.

ADVANCE PRAISE

A Field of Nopes will touch anyone who has ever put heart and brain on the line for a job—particularly those who have ever had to fend for their dignity and sanity in the brutal yet cruelly tactful academic market. These poems quietly blast through the wall of mystique surrounding rejection. Drawing from redacted official letters and other application materials, Ducat has delivered a collection that echoes the satiric tradition of Kafka and Vonnegut, the economy and wordplay of Dickinson and cummings, the lyricism of Rilke and Neruda. Readers will find here a kindred of yeses.

—**Jo Scott-Coe**, author of *Unheard Witness: The Life and Death of Kathy Leissner Whitman* (UT Press)

In this witty and brutal series of erasures, James Ducat lays bare the "rhetorical angels" of academic HR, questioning whether there's room for humans in such a machine. Ducat evokes moments of unexpected lyricism amidst the fragments of corporate-speak. Somehow, the poems open a space for "courage,/ courage in the open/ sea" of endless nopes.

—**Phoebe Reeves**, author of *Helen of Bikini* (Lily Poetry Review Books)

The eraser on a pencil is a tool of correction. The blacking/whiting out model of erasure is an annihilation. As a political tool, erasure poetry aims to unbury the missing the subtext, to reanimate the hidden de- and constructive energy of the underlying text. An adjunct's lot is hard, and the current academic field is ripe for sociopolitical reexamination. Snatching back the self from the perilous edge of rejection ("I seek I,/I am"), James Ducat's new chapbook uses erasure as engagement, taking control of the emotional possibilities of rejection and turning the offensive language of aggressively polite rejection into wry, empathic self-compassion.

—**Jenny Factor**, Finalist, Lambda Literary Award, author of *Want the Lake* (Red Hen Press) and *Unraveling at the Name* (Copper Canyon Press)

RELEASE
confidence
if you fail

I authorize pressure.

I waive my right
to be considered valid

I release
harm, damage,
or any similar result

I further expressly
waive
privacy.

I voluntarily
name others

RELEASE

confidence   if you fail

I authorize

pressure,

I   waive my right

to be considered   valid

I   release

harm,   damage,

or any similar   result
I further expressly

waive   privacy.

I   voluntarily

Name   Other   s

Name
your style
and

tell us
you
disrupt
it.

How do you engage
with irrelevant
guidelines?

Name your style and

Tell us it. you disrupt

How do you engage with guidelines ? irrelevant

July 17

Please believe
I hold a rhetorical angel

a force
a champion

free
strong
heavy
and temporary

July 17,

Please believe

I hold a Rhetoric al Angel

A
Force

A champion

free
strong

heavy
and temporary

accept appreciation
process want
appreciate impress
thank luck

accept   appreciation

interest   process   want   appreciate

impress

thank   luck

Interview Act

time and rest we all
want, but it's
a problem.

Just think,
like me,
you know
time
has
a family.

Interview Act

time and rest We all want , but it's

a problem.

Just think

like me

you know

time

has

a family.

For what will you part?

Given how
you handle
good

describe or prove
how it is
specific

How do you differ
differently?

FOR

What will you part?

Given how

you handle
good

Describe How or prove it is

specific How

Do you differ differently?

How do you
enhance demons

demons teach
corporate composition

Do you have any questions?

How do you

enhance

DEMONS

demons

Teach   corporate   Composition

Do you have any questions ?

nope.

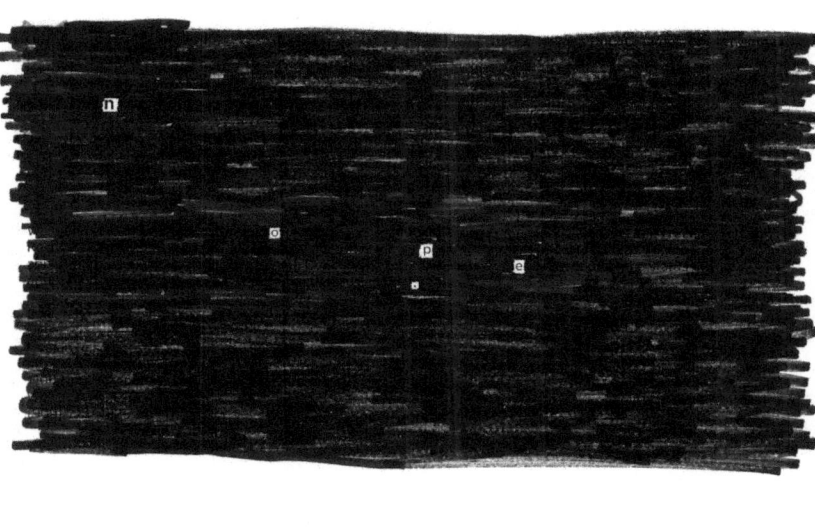

Tue, Feb 17,

Dear:

your interest will serve you
no longer.

courage,
courage in the open
sea

Tue, Feb 17,

Dear

your interest
no longer   will serve   you

courage

courage   in the   open
            sea

for your interest
Mon, Jun 2,
We unable you

for your interest

Mon, Jun 2,

We unable you

NOTICE TO APPLICANT

Form regard for
judgment
not obtained by
public record

NOTICE TO APPLICANT

FORM

regard for

judgment

NOT obtained by

public record

March 25,

Dear:

We regret that
you were not appreciated.

March 25

Dear :

We regret that

you were not appreciate

d .

July, 2,

College is pleased to announce an interment
or equivalent
OR equivalent
or equivalent
OR the equivalent

The
demons
course
from
method
to
experience.

Demons issue
stances.

Inter
them.

July, 2,

College is pleased to announce an inter ment

or equivalent
OR or equivalent equivalent
or equivalent
OR the equivalent.

The

Demons

course

from

to

method

experience.

Demons issue

stances,

Inter the m .

nope.

don't
use
I.

Know
I use
I.

I
I
I

I have been.

use don't I.

know

I use

I.

I
I
I

I have been .

Summon an oasis
of freeways.

The
body
needs,
day and night,
to smooth
responses.

Summer on AN OASIS of freeways.

the body needs,
day and night, to
smooth

Responses.

If you look
over 45,
the committee
chair will cut
you off.

What
shape
sympathy ?

What do you
know
you do not
have

If you look over
45
, the committee chair will cut you off.

What shape

sympathy

?
what do you know
do not have you

Evaluate evaluation
and evaluation.
Assign regulations
Participate by examination
Participate as needed.
Participate in the alternative
such as:
Course and course or courses,
Participate,
Participate,
Continue to
Participate,
Participate,
Participate or
Schedule and
participate,
Participate
or participate,
Participate,
Participate and
Participate as required

Evaluate evaluation and evaluation.

Assign regulations

Participate by examination

Participate as needed.
Participate in the alternative

such as:

Course and
course
or
courses

Participate

Participate
Continue to
Participate
Participate
participate or

Schedule and
participate
Participate

or participate

Participate
Participate and

Participate as required.

February 17,

Consider
a second material life
more than receptacles
to foster "His job contributions."

I seek I,
I am

February 17,

consider

a second   more   than   material
life

receptacles

to foster

"His
          job   contributions."
I seek
I

                                              , I
        am

nope.

Wed. Apr 1,

time to posit regret

this wish ends

state and address
privilege

. . . .

complete
Thu, Apr 16,
regret

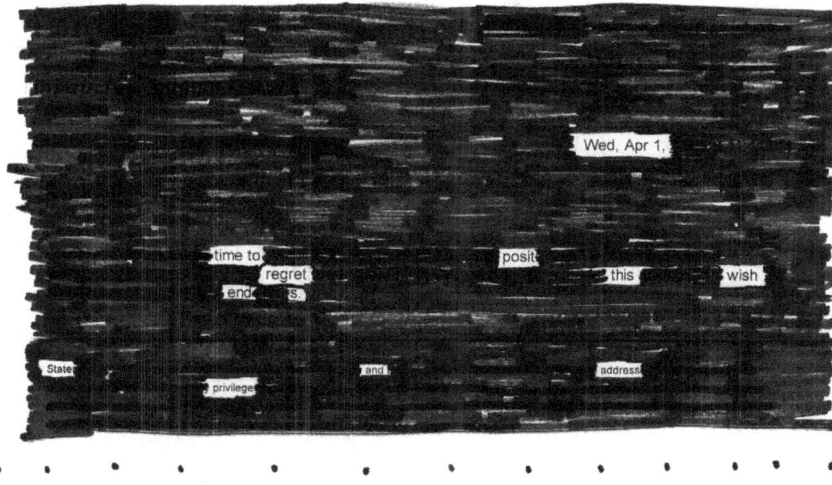

Wed, Apr 1,

time to regret posit this wish
ends.
State privilege and address

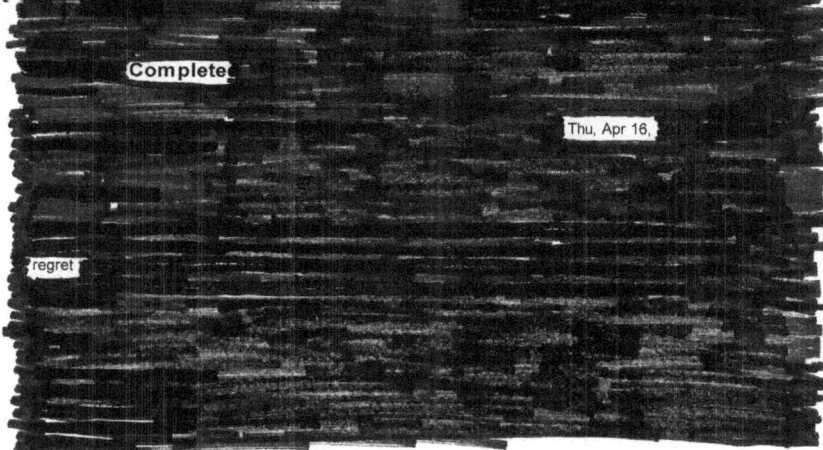

Complete

Thu, Apr 16,

regret

April 21,

Dear:

We would like to extend
our position that
you have not been
appreciated

April 21,

Dear

we would like to extend our

position

tha

you have not been   appreciated

destruction
questions
destruction

Destruction

questions

Destruction

teaching?
no longer impressive.
name drop

teaching? no longer impressive. name drop

nope.

www.ingramcontent.com/pod-product-compliance
Lightning Source LLC
Chambersburg PA
CBHW080943040426
42444CB00015B/3422